The Book of
CRYSTALS

"Awake! for Morning in the Bowl of Night

Has flung the Stone that puts the Stars to Flight."

THE RUBAIYAT OF OMAN KHAYAM

"Invest in the human soul. Who knows, it might be

a diamond in the rough."

MARY MCLEOD BETHUNE

The Book of
CRYSTALS

A PRACTICAL GUIDE TO THE BEAUTY

AND HEALING INFLUENCE OF

CRYSTALS AND GEMSTONES

LANSDOWNE

CONT

E N T S

I N T R O

DUCTION

Often described as the flowers of the mineral kingdom, crystals have fascinated humankind from the earliest times. Tales of Lemuria and Atlantis indicate that these fabled civilizations had harnessed the magical power of crystals for both practical and esoteric use and then fell because of the abuse of that awesome power.

Crystals have been found in the tombs and temples of the ancient Egyptians. References to the magical powers of stones and explanations of how crystals were formed are found throughout Greek mythology. Pliny, a naturalist of ancient Rome, meticulously recorded the properties crystals were believed to have had at the time, including their ability to replicate.

Crystals were mined and used extensively throughout the Middle Ages where they were often considered to possess magical powers and healing energies. They were frequently ground to powders and taken mixed with water as medicines.

Native Americans used at least eighty different stones before European settlement. Many of these stones were used in healing and spiritual ceremonies or carried as talismans, others were used in more practical ways.

The book of Exodus in the Bible describes the breastplate of the high priest being embedded with twelve stones, each with special properties to provide the priest with wisdom and knowledge.

Crystals were once classified only by their color and more than one stone was often given the same name. For the ancients, there was no way of distinguishing between purple fluorite and amethyst, lapis lazuli was known as "sapphire" and red stones were known as "rubies". In 1546 *De Natura Fossilium* by Georgius Agricola identified crystals and other minerals by their hardness, luster and color, a system that forms the basis of today's mineral classification.

Much of our modern day jewellery has evolved from the wearing of crystals as medicine and as amulets and talismans.

What are Crystals?

A crystal is a mineral or combination of minerals that has formed in a regular, geometric shape. Some crystals are formed when lava from the earth's core pushes its way through rock, slowly cooling. Some are the result of the fusion of minerals on the surface of the earth, while others will be formed when a mineral is placed under enormous pressure and exposed to heat deep within the earth's crust.

Quartz crystal is made from silica, one of the most commonly found compounds on earth and one of the components of the human body. A wide variety of crystals belong to the quartz family.

Types of crystals

Single Terminated Crystals

These are also called generator crystals. All faces of this crystal meet in a point at one end in what is known as a "terminated apex". The other end of the crystal was once joined to the base of a crystal cluster and may have other smaller crystals attached to it. Energy is said to flow from the crystal, out through the apex.

Double Terminated Crystals

These crystals have a terminated apex at each end of the crystal. This shows they were formed in an environment, such as soft clay, where they were able to fully develop

their natural shape. Double terminated crystals are considered powerful because their shape allows them to release energy from both ends.

CLUSTERS

A large number of crystals will often form together, joined to a single base. Once removed from their natural environment, these crystals may break into smaller clusters or individual stones.

PHANTOM CRYSTALS

Phantom crystals can display stunning "gardens" of mineral traces within a quartz crystal or there may be a smaller, ghostly image of the crystal at its center. A wide variety of colors may be displayed, depending on the mineral present.

MASSES

Some crystals do not form individual, terminated crystals but form in veins and are found in chunks and masses. Other stones that are called crystals may not, in the strict, geological sense of the word, be crystals. Amber for example is the fossilized sap of trees.

Choosing your Crystals

Receiving a crystal as a gift is always a precious experience, and as you begin to use crystals you may discover that you begin to find crystals, or rather they will "find" you. It is not uncommon for these crystals to be just what you need at that given moment. It is also not uncommon to lose crystals, and many crystal healers see this as an indication that the crystal has served its purpose in that situation and is no longer required. There will also be times when you may wish to purchase a stone and, given the great abundance of healing stones now available, it can be useful to have a system for choosing your crystals. It is possible to buy crystals by mail order or through the Internet, however there really is no substitute for being able to see, touch and feel a crystal before deciding to buy it. The best place to first buy crystals is from a store or market stall where the retailer has a genuine interest in their crystals. A good retailer will be able to tell you the general characteristics and traits of a stone, and encourage you to trust your intuition when purchasing a crystal.

Choosing by "first sight"

Often when you first see a range of crystals, one stone will catch your eye and continue to draw your attention. This is likely to be a stone that can be beneficial to you. At this point you may like to trust your intuition and purchase the crystal or you can use one of the other methods below.

If you feel overwhelmed by choice, or you are unsure of which crystal it was you saw first, try standing quietly for a few moment with your eyes closed and remember your reason for wanting to purchase a crystal. When you open your eyes, you may find there is a particular stone shining more brightly than the others — this is the one to choose.

Using a pendulum

Using a pendulum is a simple way to seek answers from your subconscious mind if you are wanting to choose a stone or crystal for healing purposes. For more information on how to use a pendulum, see USING CRYSTALS FOR PREDICTIONS, pages 74–76.

Choosing for yourself

Hold a pendulum over the top of the crystal and ask "Will this crystal be useful to me at this time?" Another way to use the pendulum, if you are considering a large number of crystals, is to pass the pendulum slowly over the top of all the crystals and look for any circular movement in the pendulum. If you do find the pendulum reacting over a particular stone it is then a good idea to hold the pendulum directly over that stone and ask a question.

Choosing for another person

Again, hold the pendulum above the crystal you are considering and, forming in your mind an image of the person you think the crystal might be useful for, ask "Will this crystal be useful to (name of person) at this time?"

Sensing crystals

All crystals vibrate at their own frequency and some people are sensitive enough to feel these vibrations. Holding or placing your hand on a large piece of clear quartz crystal is one way to develop your sensitivity to these vibrations. Sometimes a quartz may give off a regular pulse of energy; you may feel others as being cold in your hand or very warm; other crystals may produce a tingling sensation on your skin. Generally a crystal that will be beneficial to you will feel right to you even though you may not be able to describe the sensations it creates.

CARING FOR YOUR CRYSTALS

Crystals can benefit from being recharged by the energy in sunlight for a short period of time. Too much exposure to direct sunlight can fade the color from many stones. However, it makes sense to take advantage of their beauty and display them in a well-lit part of your home or office that is not in constant direct sunlight. Cleansing the stones of undesirable energies when you first acquire them and then regularly thereafter will keep the crystals energized and maintain their luster. Crystals should always be treated with care as, although hard to the touch, they can often be fragile and prone to chipping or breaking.

HANDLING CRYSTALS

UNCUT CRYSTALS AND "POINTS"

When moving uncut crystals they should be individually wrapped or placed singly in a pouch made from a natural fiber to prevent chipping and other damage.

CRYSTAL CLUSTERS

Depending on the amount of humidity in your environment and the age of the clusters, it is not uncommon for individual stones to work their way free from clusters or for a cluster to break into pieces. This may happen no matter how careful you are as it may simply be the opening of an existing fissure. However it is wise to place clusters where they are unlikely to get knocked and be gentle when handling them. Great care needs to be taken when transporting clusters.

Tumbled stones with rounded edges are fairly hardy and are the most resistant to being roughly handled. In the same way that crystal clusters may, over time, break apart, polished pieces of some stones, such as agate, may also separate into the layers that developed while they were forming.

CRYSTAL CLEANSING

There are many rituals that can be followed to cleanse crystals. Some crystals transform energies, others absorb or transmit energies. By cleansing, the intention is to clear away patterns of energy that may be undesirable or inappropriate to you while at the same time attuning the crystal's energy to your own. There are many ways in which you can cleanse the crystal and, as intention is the most important aspect, choose the method you feel most comfortable with — they are all effective.

It is not necessary to use detergent or soap on your stones unless they are visibly dirty or freshly mined, as what is required is an energy cleansing rather than a physical one and harsh detergents may effect the luster of some of the softer stones.

MOONBATH

Place the crystals in a glass or ceramic bowl filled with cold water and place it outside where it can be bathed in moonlight overnight. Full moons are an excellent time to cleanse the crystals and some people choose to make this a monthly ritual. This method is not recommended if your crystal has been set as a piece of jewelry as soaking may loosen any adhesive used. It is also not recommended for turquoise which may lose some of its color through this process.

SUNBATH

Firstly, rinse the stones under running water and then place the crystals in a position where they can catch the rays of the sun as it reaches its peak intensity around noon. Leave for an hour or so.

SEAWATER

Leave the crystals in fresh seawater or in a solution of water and sea salt for a few hours. Never use hot water to cleanse a crystal as the heat can cause the crystal to split or fracture.

MEDITATION

Use a simple meditation to visualize all negative energy flowing from the crystal with each outward breath you make. After a few minutes, imagine the crystal full of brilliant light, clean and clear.

CRYSTAL CLUSTERS AND GEODES

A cluster of crystals or a crystal geode can be used to cleanse or charge a smaller crystal. Leave the crystal for a day or so cradled in the cluster or geode. In this position, the crystal will be within the piezoelectrical field generated by the many crystals that make up the cluster.

RETURN TO THE EARTH

You may choose to return your crystals to the earth to cleanse them; this may mean burying them in a pot plant or in rich soil in your garden. If your crystal is single terminated, place with the point facing upwards. Leave for two or three days and then uncover.

BURNING SAGE

Sage has been used traditionally as a purifying herb. Burn some loose sage in a small dish or light a "smudge stick" of sage and slowly move the crystal through the smoke so that every facet of the crystal is exposed to the smoke.

CRYSTALS

A – Z

AGATE, BLUE

PHYSICAL HEALING: BLUE AGATE HAS PROPERTIES WHICH STRENGTHEN AND IMPROVE THE HEALTH OF BONE AND TISSUE IN THE BODY, AND ASSIST THE BODY IN ELIMINATING IMPURITIES FROM THE BLOOD AND TISSUE. IT IS A COOLING STONE AND CAN BE BENEFICIAL WHEN A PERSON IS FEELING FEVERISH OR WHEN THE EYES ARE RED AND SORE.

EMOTIONS: PROVIDING BALANCE BETWEEN THE PHYSICAL, EMOTIONAL, MENTAL AND SPIRITUAL, BLUE AGATE ALSO ASSISTS A PERSON TO FACE FEARS AND FIND A SENSE OF INNER PEACE.

THE COOLING PROPERTIES OF THIS BLUE STONE CAN HELP DISPEL THE HEAT OF ANGER AND NEGATIVITY.

MENTAL/SPIRITUAL GROWTH: THIS CRYSTAL ENABLES US TO ACCESS POSITIVE ASPECTS OF OURSELVES AND PROVIDES INSPIRATION TO FOLLOW OUR DREAMS. IT HELPS US BRING TO THE SURFACE OUR HIDDEN TALENTS AND ABILITIES.

CHAKRAS: BALANCES THROAT AND HEART CHAKRAS.

ZODIAC AFFINITIES: PISCES, GEMINI.

Blue agate with white lace patterns is a type of chalcedony and is believed to be one of the stones embedded in the breastplate of the high priest during the time of the Old Testament. It is found in nodules or geodes, although it is often available in "slices" or cut and polished into obelisks or pyramids. Agate was commonly used during Roman times, powdered and mixed with water to counter snake bites. In twelfth-century France it was placed in the drinking and cooking vessels of those who were suffering ill health and in thirteenth-century England it was considered to be useful for strengthening sight and ensuring fidelity. Agate will act to strengthen the properties of other stones.

AMETHYST

PHYSICAL HEALING: HAVING THE PARADOXICAL ATTRIBUTES OF BEING BOTH STIMULATING AND CALMING, AMETHYSTS ACT TO RELIEVE THE EFFECTS OF STRESS AND TO STIMULATE A SLUGGISH CIRCULATORY SYSTEM. IT IS OFTEN RECOMMENDED TO THOSE WHO SUFFER FROM RESTLESS SLEEP OR INSOMNIA THAT A PIECE OF AMETHYST BE PLACED UNDER THEIR PILLOW AT NIGHT OR RUBBED LIGHTLY OVER THE TEMPLES ON RETIRING.

EMOTIONS: ABLE TO DISPEL FEARS, AMETHYST CAN ALSO SOOTHE RAGE AND EASE THE GRIEVING PROCESS. AMETHYST CAN PROVIDE CLARITY AND BALANCE WHERE EMOTIONS MAY HAVE BECOME CONFUSED AND OVERWHELMING. THE PURPLE OF AMETHYST CAN BE SOOTHING IF THE EMOTIONS SEEM UNSTABLE, SWINGING FROM ONE MOOD TO ANOTHER.

AMETHYST HELPS US TO THINK BEYOND OUR OWN, EVERYDAY NEEDS TO HIGHER IDEALS AND A SENSE OF WHAT IS BENEFICIAL TO THE WHOLE COMMUNITY.

MENTAL/SPIRITUAL GROWTH: THIS IS AN EXCELLENT CRYSTAL FOR THOSE WHO MEDITATE OR FOR THOSE WISHING TO LEARN MEDITATION AS IT INDUCES A STATE OF TRANQUILLITY AND CALM IN THE MIND. AMETHYST ALSO ASSISTS THE USER TO MORE EASILY CHANGE ADDICTIVE BEHAVIOR AND NEGATIVE BELIEFS WHILE MAKING GOALS AND DREAMS CLEARER AND MORE REALISTIC.

CHAKRAS: OPENS AND BALANCES THIRD EYE (BROW) AND CROWN CHAKRAS.

ZODIAC AFFINITIES: SAGITTARIUS, PISCES, CAPRICORN.

BIRTHSTONE: FEBRUARY.

A member of the quartz family of crystals, amethyst forms six-sided terminated crystals ranging in color from the palest of mauves to deep, almost black, purples. Until recent times it was considered a rare and precious gem used in the rings of kings and bishops and the necklaces of queens. During the Middle Ages its rarity and beauty made it more expensive than diamonds, however, large deposits found in South America have made amethyst one of the more common crystals. This abundance of single stones, clusters or geodes has made amethyst a very affordable crystal with the darker stones considered of greater value than paler stones.

Amethyst was traditionally believed to protect the wearer from intoxication and any excess of physical passion. Matrons in ancient Rome believed that a gift of amethyst to their husbands would ensure his love and fidelity. Pieces of amethyst were often given to those who were soon to face great danger or set out upon a long journey as it was considered to have a strong protective quality.

According to Greek mythology, Bacchus, the god of wine, fell in love with a young nymph who turned to the goddess Diana for protection from his unwanted attention. In desperation, Diana turned the nymph into a quartz crystal to save her, and Bacchus, saddened by the result of his actions, poured wine over the stone in the memory of his love. Thus, amethyst was created.

AQUAMARINE

PHYSICAL HEALING: AQUAMARINE STRENGTHENS AND TONES THE ORGANS AND SKELETON OF THE BODY. IT IMPROVES VISION AND RELIEVES TIRED EYES, AND CAN BENEFIT THOSE WHO SUFFER REGULARLY WITH SORE OR IRRITATED THROATS. HEADACHES, PARTICULARLY THOSE CAUSED BY TENSION OR CLENCHING THE JAW, CAN ALSO BE RELIEVED WITH THE USE OF THE AQUAMARINE.

EMOTIONS: A CALMING CRYSTAL, AQUAMARINE INDUCES CLARITY OF MIND AND AN UNDERSTANDING OF THE EMOTIONS PARTICULARLY WHEN THERE IS A FEELING OF BEING BURDENED BY RESPONSIBILITY. IT CAN BE BENEFICIAL TO THOSE WHO NEED TO LEARN TO SPEAK THEIR MIND AND OUTWARDLY EXPRESS THEIR EMOTIONS.

MENTAL/SPIRITUAL GROWTH: AQUAMARINE STIMULATES COMMUNICATION AND CLEARER SELF-EXPRESSION. IT ENCOURAGES TOLERANCE AND THE RELEASE OF JUDGMENTAL BEHAVIOR. THIS IS A VALUABLE STONE FOR MEDITATION AS IT HEIGHTENS MENTAL CLARITY, CALMS THE NERVES AND DISSIPATES FEARS.

CHAKRAS: STIMULATES THROAT AND BROW CHAKRAS.

ZODIAC AFFINITIES: GEMINI, AQUARIUS, ARIES.

BIRTHSTONE: MARCH.

The name of this crystal comes from the Latin for "sea water" which is reflected in the color of this stone, varying from light blue to green. Aquamarine is a variety of beryl, as is the emerald, and can often be found in large single crystals. Traditionally it is thought to have protected seafarers and those in battle.

AVENTURINE

PHYSICAL HEALING: ALTHOUGH USEFUL FOR ALL PARTS OF THE BODY, AVENTURINE IS PARTICULARLY BENEFICIAL FOR CONDITIONS AROUND THE HEART AND LUNG AREA. WOUNDS AND INFECTIONS BENEFIT FROM AVENTURINE WHICH IS ALSO USEFUL WHEREVER NEW MUSCLE OR SKIN TISSUE IS BEING GENERATED.

EMOTIONS: AVENTURINE IS A REJUVENATING AND SOOTHING STONE; IT ASSISTS THE PROCESS OF SELF-ACCEPTANCE AND ENCOURAGES US TO FIND TIME TO NURTURE THE SELF.

IT IS A CRYSTAL CONNECTED WITH FEELINGS OF BALANCE, CONTENTMENT AND JOY, AND OF BEING RECEPTIVE AND SINCERE.

MENTAL/SPIRITUAL GROWTH: AVENTURINE BALANCES THE MALE AND THE FEMALE ENERGIES WITHIN US AND ASSISTS UNDERSTANDING IN RELATIONSHIPS BETWEEN MEN AND WOMEN.

CHAKRAS: SOOTHES AND OPENS THE HEART CHAKRA.

ZODIAC AFFINITIES: ARIES, CANCER, LIBRA.

 Aventurine is a non-crystalline stone and although it can be found in a variety of colors, including blue and a reddish brown, it is the cool green stone that is generally recognized. Flecks of mica embedded in the stone gives it a sparkling quality. Before jade was commonly used in China, aventurine was used for carving and ornamentation. It has long been considered an all-purpose healing stone and promotes general health and well-being.

AZURITE

PHYSICAL HEALING: AZURITE HAS A RELAXING AND CALMING EFFECT ON THE NERVOUS SYSTEM AND A CLEANSING AND STRENGTHENING EFFECT ON CIRCULATION. ITS PROPERTIES ARE HEIGHTENED WHEN IT IS IN COMBINATION WITH MALACHITE.

EMOTIONS: AZURITE ENABLES US TO MORE EASILY RECOGNIZE AND RELEASE PATTERNS OF BEHAVIOR THAT ARE NO LONGER APPROPRIATE OR HELPFUL TO US AND TO DISPEL NEGATIVE THOUGHTS SURROUNDING THESE. IT HELPS US FEEL MORE DETACHED FROM EXTERNAL FORCES AND MORE CONNECTED WITH OUR INNER SELVES.

MENTAL/SPIRITUAL GROWTH: AZURITE IS BENEFICIAL TO THOSE WHO WISH TO DEVELOP THEIR PSYCHIC ABILITIES AND TO THOSE WHO WISH TO JOURNEY INTO THEMSELVES THROUGH MEDITATION. AZURITE ASSISTS IN THE DEVELOPMENT OF INTUITION AND PERSONAL INSIGHT. IT HELPS DISPEL PROCRASTINATION, GENERATING A STRONGER SENSE OF SELF-DISCIPLINE.

CHAKRAS: STIMULATES THE BROW CHAKRA.

ZODIAC AFFINITIES: SAGITTARIUS, AQUARIUS.

Light to deep blue in color, azurite forms clear, prism-shaped crystals. It is one of the stones that could go through a process called pseudomorphous. This is when one mineral replaces another without altering the form of the original mineral. Azurite is copper carbonate and in its natural state has a very low concentration of water; but if it absorbs water it changes from a translucent blue crystal to an opaque green stone called malachite. Malachite is often found as stalagmites and stalactites. Combinations of the stones are common and can occur in extremely large pieces. The Mayans are believed to have used azurite to carry and transfer knowledge and wisdom and it was also considered a powerful stone by Native Americans and Tibetans.

CARNELIAN

PHYSICAL HEALING: CARNELIAN IS A WARMING, STIMULATING STONE AND IS USEFUL WHENEVER THE BODY NEEDS WARMTH TO HEAL. THE INFLUENCE OF CARNELIAN ACTS TO STRENGTHEN THE BLOOD AND WILL WORK TO INCREASE CIRCULATION.

EMOTIONS: THE BOLDNESS OF CARNELIAN'S RICH COLOR DISPELS FEAR AND BUILDS COURAGE. CARNELIAN UPLIFTS THE EMOTIONS AND HELPS US STAY IN THE PRESENT INSTEAD OF WORRYING ABOUT THE PAST OR THE POSSIBILITIES OF THE FUTURE. IT IS A STONE THAT STRENGTHENS THE BONDS OF FAMILY.

MENTAL/SPIRITUAL GROWTH: CARNELIAN IS ALSO STIMULATING ON A MENTAL PLANE AND ASSISTS IN MAINTAINING CONCENTRATION AND CLARITY OF MIND. IT DISPELS NEGATIVITY AND CAN INCREASE OUR INNER STRENGTH AND CAPACITY FOR COMPASSION.

CHAKRAS: STIMULATES BASE AND SOLAR PLEXUS CHAKRAS.

ZODIAC AFFINITIES: TAURUS, CANCER AND LEO.

BIRTHSTONE: JULY.

A type of chalcedony, ranging in color from pale apricot through deep orange and orange/brown to orange/red, carnelian is believed to be one of the stones found in the breastplate of the high priest during biblical times. Until the end of the Middle Ages, Carnelian was ground into a powder and mixed with water to be taken internally as protection against plague; it was also considered useful as a treatment for disorders of the blood.

CHRYSOPRASE

PHYSICAL HEALING: CHRYSOPRASE IS SAID TO BE BENEFICIAL TO THE HEART, STRENGTHENING AND TONING THIS MUSCLE. IT ALSO INCREASES CIRCULATION AND CAN SOOTHE INFLAMED EYES.

EMOTIONS: THIS STONE LIFTS THE EMOTIONS AND PROVIDES RELIEF FROM DEPRESSION. CHRYSOPRASE CAN BE DESCRIBED AS A LIGHT-HEARTED STONE WHICH INDUCES WITHIN US A FEELING OF EASE WITH OUR PRESENT CIRCUMSTANCES AND RELIEF FROM RESTLESSNESS.

MENTAL/SPIRITUAL GROWTH: CHRYSOPRASE IS A STONE OF ACCEPTANCE, BOTH OF THOSE AROUND US AND OF OURSELVES. IT BRINGS WITH IT A SENSE OF PEACE, HARMONY AND BALANCE.

CHAKRAS: STIMULATES AND OPENS THE HEART CHAKRA.

ZODIAC AFFINITIES: LIBRA, PISCES.

BIRTHSTONE: MAY.

The word chrysoprase comes from the Greek for "golden green" and chrysoprase ranges in color from pale lemon green to a bright apple green. It is believed to have been one of the stones embedded in the walls of the Holy City of Jerusalem in biblical times and has been prized for centuries for its delicate color. Although generally not used for carvings because of its fragile nature, it was often used in mosaics. The color can pale if exposed to bright sunlight for long periods, but is said to return if the crystal is buried for a period of time. It is a form of opaque chalcedony and its color is due to the presence of nickel silicates during its formation.

CITRINE

PHYSICAL HEALING: CITRINE IS BENEFICIAL TO THE KIDNEYS, BLADDER AND URINARY TRACT AND CAN ALSO ASSIST WITH DIGESTIVE PROBLEMS.

EMOTIONS: CITRINE RELIEVES SELF-DESTRUCTIVE BEHAVIOR AND CREATES A SENSE OF CLARITY WITHIN.

MENTAL/SPIRITUAL GROWTH: THIS CRYSTAL WILL ENCOURAGE ELIMINATION OF THOSE THINGS IN OUR LIVES THAT NO LONGER SERVE US WELL, CREATING SPACE FOR CHANGE AND GROWTH. CITRINE ENCOURAGES THE MANIFESTATION OF OUR DREAMS.

CHAKRAS: STIMULATES THE SOLAR PLEXUS CHAKRA.

ZODIAC AFFINITIES: LIBRA AND LEO.

Most commonly found as "points" or in clusters, citrine forms six-sided terminations. Also known as "yellow quartz", true citrine is generally rarer than that which is artificially created by heating amethyst or smoky quartz to high temperatures. The fabricated stone often has a reddish tinge and may have streaks through the stone. Naturally occurring citrine is clear quartz crystal, colored by iron, that has at some point been exposed to extremely high temperatures below the earth's surface. Citrine is often imitated and, in turn, has often been cut and polished to imitate the rarer and more expensive topaz. Citrine is a stone of abundance and prosperity and is often recommended to those who feel they have difficulty attracting these qualities into their lives.

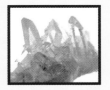

CLEAR QUARTZ

PHYSICAL HEALING: CLEAR QUARTZ CRYSTAL, WHEN HELD IN THE HAND, HAS BEEN SHOWN, THROUGH THE USE OF KIRLIAN PHOTOGRAPHY, TO INCREASE THE AMOUNT OF ENERGY AROUND THE BODY. WHEN PLACED IN A SPECIFIC AREA, IT WILL INCREASE THE AMOUNT OF ENERGY AT THAT PARTICULAR PLACE. CLEAR QUARTZ HAS THE ABILITY TO ABSORB, TRANSFORM AND TRANSMIT ENERGY MAKING THIS A VERSATILE HEALING TOOL. IT HAS THE ABILITY TO REDUCE PAIN, BOOST THE IMMUNE SYSTEM, CLEAR CONGESTION AND BLOCKAGES AND RELIEVE FATIGUE AND LETHARGY.

EMOTIONS: BALANCING AND PROVIDING ENERGY, QUARTZ STABILIZES OUR EMOTIONS AND ENCOURAGES A POSITIVE, PURPOSEFUL OUTLOOK ON LIFE.

MENTAL/SPIRITUAL GROWTH: CLEAR QUARTZ CRYSTAL CAN BE USED TO AMPLIFY OUR MENTAL PROCESSES; IT WILL BRING STRONGER, CLEARER MEDITATIONS AND CAN HEIGHTEN OUR MENTAL CLARITY. CONNECTING THE PHYSICAL, EMOTIONAL, MENTAL AND SPIRITUAL ASPECTS, CLEAR QUARTZ CAN PROVIDE A SENSE OF OVERVIEW, A NEW UNDERSTANDING OF WHAT IS TRULY IMPORTANT TO US, AND WHAT IS SUPERFICIAL.

CHAKRAS: STIMULATES AND BALANCES ALL CHAKRAS.

ZODIAC AFFINITIES: QUARTZ HAS AN AFFINITY WITH ALL ASTROLOGICAL SIGNS.

During the Middle Ages, clear quartz crystal was often mistaken for diamonds; it was also used to reduce fevers by placing it on the tongue. This crystal's cooling property was also recognized by the ancient Romans who carried spheres of quartz as a means of keeping their hands cool during the heat of the summer months. Also known as rock crystal, the ancient Greeks believed that clear quartz was formed when mountains applied pressure and cold to the water flowing between them. Quartz has the ability to produce electricity when under pressure by mechanical force or heat, or by the application of sound waves. Thin slices of quartz can be used to transmit exact frequencies of sound waves by grinding the slices down to a precise thickness. This piezoelectric quality has made clear quartz a valuable tool in technology so it is used extensively in the telecommunications and electronics industries.

Clear quartz has been considered a powerful stone by many cultures throughout the world and was used by the indigenous people of northern Australia to initiate rain, in Persia to ensure a nursing mother had a plentiful supply of breast milk, by the Cherokee for divination, and in the Shetland Islands quartz pebbles were collected to increase fertility.

As a healing stone today, clear quartz is considered one of the most powerful. It will also act to amplify the effect of any other crystal. Quartz is formed primarily of silicic acid, a substance that is also found in our spines and in our eyes — perhaps this is the reason quartz seems to resonate with the human body.

Other types of quartz

Amethyst, rose quartz, smoky quartz and citrine, agate, chrysoprase, aventurine, obsidian and jasper are all quartz crystals with the addition of various minerals that were present where the crystals were formed. Quartz also forms within other substances and will, for example, replace the fibers in wood, maintaining the shape and colorings, producing petrified wood. Tiger's eye is another example, where quartz has replaced asbestos fibers.

Rutilated quartz contains hairlike needles of gold, yellow, red or black formed by the presence of titanium. Often called "angel's hair" or "Venus' hair", these crystals are prized for their beauty. Rutilated smoky quartz can also be found and the presence of the needles act to enhance the healing qualities of both clear and smoky quartz.

FLUORITE

PHYSICAL HEALING: THE ATTRIBUTES OF FLUORITE ARE SO OFTEN FOCUSED ON THE INTELLECT, THAT ITS PHYSICAL HEALING PROPERTIES ARE SOMETIMES OVERLOOKED. IT ASSISTS THE BODY BY THE CLEANSING AND REJUVENATION OF CELLS AND IS BELIEVED TO STRENGTHEN THE BODY'S NATURAL RESISTANCE TO DISEASE, BOOSTING THE IMMUNE SYSTEM. THE VARIOUS COLORS OF FLUORITE WILL EACH HAVE ITS OWN EFFECT, THE COOLING OF BLUE FLUORITE, FOR INSTANCE, IS CONSIDERED USEFUL IN REDUCING THE HEAT OF INFLAMMATIONS, AND YELLOW FLUORITE WILL ASSIST THE LIVER IN THE ELIMINATION OF FAT AND TOXINS FROM THE BODY.

EMOTIONS: FLUORITE HELPS RECONNECT US TO A SENSE OF INNER PEACE AND SERENITY, ENABLING GREATER SYNERGY BETWEEN THE MIND AND THE EMOTIONS. BLUE FLUORITE WILL COOL THE HEAT OF ANGER, GREEN AND PURPLE FLUORITE WILL INDUCE US TO MORE FREELY EXPRESS LOVE AND AFFECTION AND CLEAR FLUORITE WILL HAVE A BALANCING EFFECT ON THE EMOTIONS.

MENTAL/SPIRITUAL GROWTH: MEDITATIONS WITH FLUORITE ENHANCE MENTAL CLARITY FOCUS. IT CAN BE USEFUL IF YOU ARE SEARCHING FOR AN ANSWER OR FOR INSIGHT INTO A LONG-STANDING PROBLEM. FLUORITE IS A GOOD CHOICE FOR SOMEONE STARTING TO PRACTICE MEDITATION AS IT WILL HELP LENGTHEN THE TIME OF THE MEDITATIVE STATE. FLUORITE HAS THE ADDED EFFECT OF REJUVENATING THE MIND AFTER EXPENDING MENTAL ENERGY AND HELPS US MAINTAIN CLARITY IN MENTALLY TIRING SITUATIONS. AN IDEAL STONE FOR ANYONE WHO WORKS OR STUDIES UNDER MENTAL PRESSURE.

CHAKRAS: THE COMBINATION OF CLEAR, GREEN AND PURPLE WITHIN ONE CRYSTAL IS HIGHLY REGARDED BY MANY HEALERS. THE CLEAR STIMULATES THE CROWN CHAKRA, THE GREEN OPENS THE HEART CHAKRA AND THE PURPLE ACTIVATES THE BROW CHAKRA, CREATING SYNERGY BETWEEN INTELLECT, INTUITION AND SPIRITUALITY.

ZODIAC AFFINITIES: PISCES AND CAPRICORN.

Fluorite is generally a translucent stone and can be found with a large variety of colors through the stone. White, pink, purple, green and blue predominate and combinations of colors are often found with spectacular patterns and variations of color. Some specimens of fluorite have the fascinating quality of being fluorescent. This is not a consistent quality however and it is even possible to find a fluorescent crystal within a non-fluorescent piece of fluorite.

Fluorite is one of the few stones to form octahedrons, and the eight sides of the individual stones can be viewed as two pyramid shapes back to back. These individual crystals may also be found joined into a cluster.

Because of the variety of colors and color combinations of fluorite available, some healers may work solely with fluorite, using a different colored piece at each chakra for balance and alignment of the body's energy.

HEMATITE

PHYSICAL HEALING: TRADITIONALLY HEMATITE IS ASSOCIATED WITH THE BLOOD, LOWERING BLOOD PRESSURE, IMPROVING CIRCULATION AND THE QUALITY OF THE BLOOD, PREVENTING EXCESSIVE BLEEDING DURING CHILDBIRTH AND STEMMING THE FLOW OF BLOOD FROM WOUNDS.

EMOTIONS: DEFLECTING NEGATIVITY AND DISPELLING FEARS, HEMATITE REDUCES PAINFUL EMOTIONS AND EASES OUR REACTIONS TO STRESS. CALMING AND SOOTHING, IT CAN HELP THOSE AT A POINT OF NERVOUS EXHAUSTION TO FIND RESTFUL SLEEP.

MENTAL/SPIRITUAL GROWTH: HEMATITE CAN PROVIDE BALANCE BETWEEN THE PHYSICAL, THE EMOTIONAL AND THE MENTAL. IT ENCOURAGES AND STRENGTHENS THE CONNECTION BETWEEN THE LOGICAL MIND AND INTUITION.

CHAKRAS: BALANCES THE BASE CHAKRA.

ZODIAC AFFINITIES: ARIES AND AQUARIUS.

Hematite is a shiny, heavy stone that looks and feels very similar to metal. Ranging from a steel grey to silvery black in color, it is sometimes found with a red flash within the stone. It takes its name from the Greek word for blood and in some countries is known as "bloodstone". This sometimes causes confusion between this stone and the stone more commonly known as bloodstone which is a dark green jasper with red spots. Hematite has been considered since ancient Greek and Roman times as a stone that protects against wounds and other dangers, instilling courage and strength in the wearer. It was also thought to maintain these qualities during childbirth, giving endurance and strength and preventing heavy bleeding.

JADE

PHYSICAL HEALING: ALL JADE IS BENEFICIAL TO THE KIDNEYS, DIGESTIVE SYSTEM AND THE HEART, BUT THE HEALING QUALITIES OF JADE ARE ALSO LINKED TO THE COLOR OF THE STONE:

BLUE JADE HAS A CALMING QUALITY AND SOOTHES THE MIND AND THE EMOTIONS. ITS VIBRATION OPENS OUR MINDS TO THE PEACE WITHIN US, WHICH MAKES IT AN EXCELLENT MEDITATION STONE.

RED JADE IS A POWERFUL STONE; ITS STIMULATING COLOR ENABLES US TO ACCESS THE MORE VOLATILE ASPECTS OF OUR NATURE. IF ANGER AND PENT-UP ENERGY IS RESTRICTING YOUR ACTIONS, RED JADE CAN HELP RELIEVE THE TENSION BY INITIATING THE EXPRESSION OF THESE EMOTIONS.

LAVENDER JADE BRINGS EMOTIONAL BALANCE, IT ENCOURAGES THE EXPRESSION OF UNCONDITIONAL LOVE AND ENABLES GREATER FEELINGS OF SELF-ACCEPTANCE.

YELLOW JADE STIMULATES THE SOLAR PLEXUS CHAKRA, IMPROVES A SLUGGISH DIGESTIVE SYSTEM AND TONES THE LIVER.

EMOTIONS: WITH ITS CALMING AND BALANCING INFLUENCES, JADE CAN BE USEFUL TO THOSE TRYING TO RESOLVE CONFLICT — EITHER WITHIN THEMSELVES OR WITH ANOTHER PERSON. JADE IS A STONE THAT ILLICITS LOVE WHICH CAN THEN BE MORE EASILY AND MORE READILY EXPRESSED.

MENTAL/SPIRITUAL GROWTH: JADE ENABLES US TO TRANSCEND THE PRESSURES OF OUR PHYSICAL NEEDS AND FOCUS ON HIGHER IDEALS. IT OPENS UP A GREATER AWARENESS OF THE NEEDS OF THOSE AROUND US AND GENERATES THE COMPASSION AND CONFIDENCE TO INITIATE CHANGE.

CHAKRAS: BLUE STIMULATES THE THROAT CHAKRA; LAVENDER AND GREEN JADE BALANCES THE HEART CHAKRAS; WHITE JADE OPENS THE CROWN CHAKRA; YELLOW OR RED JADE STIMULATES THE BELLY AND SOLAR PLEXUS CHAKRAS.

ZODIAC AFFINITIES: LIBRA, GEMINI, TAURUS.

A non-crystalline stone, jade is found in a wide variety of colors: white, brown, lavender, salmon pink, blue and yellow. It is, of course, also found in every shade of green. Throughout the centuries many cultures have recognized jade's curative and spiritual significance. In Asia, it is considered a stone of good fortune and is often worn as an amulet. In times past, it was believed that a cup made from jade would crack if it came into contact with poison. The Maori of New Zealand carve *hei-tikis* from jade which are passed from generation to generation, connecting the wearer to their ancestors. Traditionally in China, Egypt and Mexico, a small piece of jade was placed in the mouth of those who had died. It represented the heart which was often buried or preserved separately from the rest of the body. In China it was also usual for all orifices of the body of the deceased to be covered with pieces of jade to prevent demons and evil spirits entering the body.

In several cultures jade was considered to have healing properties effective for kidney infections and kidney stones. A beautiful stone, it was generally worn in decorative jewelry, even when being used therapeutically, but could also be taken ground into a powder and mixed with water.

In old China jade was believed to be pure water from the mountains that had crystallized — its powers were considered far reaching. If taken in sufficient quantities, jade could bestow immortality; smaller quantities could provide an extended youth, vitality, good health, fertility and wisdom. It was believed to strengthen muscle and bone and relieve the body of its need for food, water or warmth.

Jade produces a beautifully rich and resonant tone when struck lightly and gongs of jade have been used in China, Africa and by the Hopi tribe of Arizona.

Jade is similar to turquoise in that it is said to lose its color and luster if its wearer is facing imminent danger or ill health.

JASPER

PHYSICAL HEALING: JASPER TONES AND STRENGTHENS THE INTERNAL ORGANS AND HELPS THE BODY DEAL WITH EXPOSURE TO POLLUTANTS.

EMOTIONS: JASPER IS A STONE THAT REMINDS US OF THE NEED TO TAKE CARE OF OURSELVES, EMOTIONALLY AS WELL AS PHYSICALLY. IT IS A STONE OF SELF-ACCEPTANCE AND IT DEEPENS SELF-AWARENESS.

MENTAL/SPIRITUAL GROWTH: A PRACTICAL CRYSTAL, JASPER HELPS US DIRECT OUR MENTAL ABILITIES INTO ACTION. JASPER STIMULATES THE IMAGINATION AND ENABLES US TO ACCESS OUR DREAMS THROUGH MEDITATION.

CHAKRAS: JASPER ALIGNS ALL THE CHAKRAS; IN ADDITION, RED JASPER OPENS THE BASE CHAKRA; BLACK, TAN AND GRAY VARIETIES CALM THE BASE CHAKRA; YELLOW JASPER STIMULATES THE SOLAR PLEXUS CHAKRA; GREEN BALANCES THE HEART CHAKRA.

ZODIAC AFFINITIES: LEO.

Jasper is an opaque quartz and comes in a wide variety of colors and color combinations, it can include shades of red, green, gray, yellow, black, and tan. Used during the Middle Ages as an amulet against witchcraft, the curative powers of jasper were written about in England and Europe as early as the eleventh century. It was attributed with the power to improve digestion and appetite, cure epilepsy, prevent kidney stones and counteract the effects of snake venom. Bloodstone, a dark green jasper with spots of blood-red iron oxide, was used during these times to stop the flow of blood.

Today jasper is often found as tumbled stones, beads or cut and polished in spheres or obelisks. The name "picture jasper" is usually given to stones with a combination of earthy tones forming a "landscape". There are many other names, often varying from place to place, given to the many different color combinations of jasper.

LABRADORITE

PHYSICAL HEALING: LABRADORITE IS SAID TO INCREASE THE OVERALL EFFICIENCY OF THE BODY'S METABOLISM. IT ALSO IMPROVES THE FUNCTION OF THE DIGESTIVE SYSTEM AND THE ELIMINATION OF TOXINS AND WASTE PRODUCTS FROM THE BODY. LIKE MANY OTHER BLUE STONES, IT IS ALSO BELIEVED TO IMPROVE VISION AND DISORDERS OF THE EYES.

EMOTIONS: THIS CRYSTAL ENCOURAGES US TO LET GO OF THE OLD — BEHAVIOR PATTERNS, HABITS, ANXIETIES, GRUDGES, BELIEFS, PREJUDICES — AND MOTIVATE US TO FIND INNOVATIVE WAYS TO ATTAIN OUR DREAMS AND DESIRES.

MENTAL/SPIRITUAL GROWTH: LABRADORITE ENABLES OUR THINKING MINDS TO PUT INTO ACTION MESSAGES FROM OUR INTUITION. STIMULATING OUR MENTAL PROCESSES AND ENHANCING OUR ABILITY FOR RATIONAL THOUGHT, LABRADORITE HELPS US DISTINGUISH BETWEEN THOUGHTS THAT HAVE THEIR BASIS IN FEAR, ANGER AND IGNORANCE FROM THOSE THAT HAVE THEIR BASIS IN COMPASSION, UNDERSTANDING AND RESPONSIBILITY FOR SELF.

CHAKRAS: BALANCES THE THROAT CHAKRA AND STIMULATES THE BROW CHAKRA.

ZODIAC AFFINITIES: SAGITTARIUS AND SCORPIO.

Also known as spectrolite, labradorite is a form of feldspar and displays brilliant reflections of vivid blues, coppery reds and golds due to the formation of thin plates in the stone's composition that split and reflect the light. When the stone is turned to catch the light even more colors become visible, similar to the way in which an opal displays its colors. Labradorite was traditionally worn as a talisman, protecting its wearer from evil and misfortune.

LAPIS LAZULI

PHYSICAL HEALING: LAPIS LAZULI IS USEFUL IN EVERY ASPECT OF HEALING: IT CAN REDUCE PAIN, IT IS A TONIC TO THE NERVOUS SYSTEM, IT COOLS WHERE THERE IS INFLAMMATION AND SWELLING, AND IT SUPPORTS THE BODY'S OWN HEALING BY BOOSTING THE IMMUNE SYSTEM. IT ALSO INDUCES DEEP AND SOUND SLEEP.

EMOTIONS: LAPIS LAZULI INSPIRES POSITIVE THINKING AND CAN HELP LIFT MILD DEPRESSION AND BAD MOODS. IT IS ALSO A STONE FOR SELF-CONFIDENCE AND SELF-EXPRESSION AND CAN GENERATE ENCOURAGEMENT TO THOSE WHO FIND IT DIFFICULT TO SPEAK OUT.

MENTAL/SPIRITUAL GROWTH: A STONE OF COMMUNITY AND SOCIAL RESPONSIBILITY, LAPIS LAZULI ENCOURAGES US TO WORK FOR THE GREATER GOOD BY CONNECTING THE SPIRITUAL WITH THE PHYSICAL. IT IS A CRYSTAL THAT HEIGHTENS AWARENESS AND SENSITIVITY AND CAN AWAKEN THE "THIRD EYE", BRINGING FORTH PSYCHIC DEVELOPMENT AND INSIGHT.

CHAKRAS: OPENS THE BROW AND THROAT CHAKRAS.

ZODIAC AFFINITIES: ARIES, TAURUS AND AQUARIUS.

BIRTHSTONE: SEPTEMBER.

The "sapphire of the ancients", lapis lazuli has been highly regarded since ancient Egyptian times when is was inlaid into their highly decorated furniture and carved into great pillars and decorative items. It is an opaque stone and its midnight blue coloring suggested to the ancient Egyptians that it was a stone from the heavens; the flecks of mica or pyrites contained within it were seen as representing the stars in the night sky.

The modern name of this stone comes from a combination of the Latin for stone, *lapis*, and the Persian word for blue, *lazure*, although in ancient times when stones were named by their color rather than their chemical composition it was referred to as sapphire.

Lapis lazuli has always been linked to the spiritual. The ancient Egyptians used lapis lazuli in their temples; it was one of the stones in the breastplate of the high priest of Israel; the tables upon which Moses received the Law were made of lapis lazuli; and it was used in altars in Spanish churches.

Powdered lapis has been used both medicinally and practically for centuries. It was used to dye cloth for the robes of nobility and the high officials of the church and as a draught to purge melancholy. It is also the base of the pigment ultramarine that is available only to the finest artists and to the very wealthy.

Although lapis is rarely found in the massive pieces of ancient times, it is commonly available in smaller pieces, and forms in masses and cubes. Its granular structure means that it is a softer stone than many and does not polish to a high luster. Although still held in high esteem for its rich color, in small pieces it is an affordable stone.

MALACHITE

PHYSICAL HEALING: THE GREEN OF MALACHITE IS THE COLOR OF SPRING AND THIS STONE ASSISTS WHEREVER REJUVENATION IS REQUIRED; WHETHER IT IS BROKEN BONES OR INJURIES TO MUSCLE AND SKIN, MALACHITE WILL SUPPORT THE BODIES INNATE HEALING POWERS. MALACHITE ALSO ACTS AS A CLEANSING STONE AND IMPROVES THE QUALITY OF THE BLOOD AND ASSISTS THE BODY IN REMOVING TOXINS AND WASTE PRODUCTS. IT STRENGTHENS AND SOOTHES THE NERVOUS SYSTEM, MAKING IT A USEFUL STONE IF NERVOUS TENSION IS CREATING OR AGGRAVATING HEALTH PROBLEMS.

EMOTIONS: MALACHITE IS A STONE OF BALANCE AND CAN FACILITATE A CALMING OF EMOTIONS, PARTICULARLY WHEN AN UNCOMFORTABLE EMOTION HAS BEEN DOMINATING OR IS BEING EXPRESSED IN A PAINFUL OR INAPPROPRIATE WAY.

MENTAL/SPIRITUAL GROWTH: WHEN USED IN MEDITATION, MALACHITE'S BALANCING NATURE ENABLES US TO SEE CLEARLY BOTH THE DESIRABLE AND LESS DESIRABLE PARTS OF OURSELVES. THIS CAN BE A POWERFUL CATALYST FOR CHANGE WHEN WE ARE FEELING READY FOR CHANGE, BUT CAN BE DISTRESSING IF WE ARE FEELING VULNERABLE, SO MALACHITE IS BEST USED INITIALLY FOR SHORT MEDITATIONS.

CHAKRAS: OPENS HEART AND THROAT CHAKRAS.

ZODIAC AFFINITIES: ARIES AND AQUARIUS.

BIRTHSTONE: SEPTEMBER.

Malachite is a hydrated form of azurite and is often found with azurite. It ranges from light to dark green and many shades may be found in the one piece of stone, in fact a stone of solid color is rarely found. Dust particles from malachite are toxic if inhaled or ingested so it is always safest to use a polished stone rather than an uncut piece.

Malachite was used extensively in ancient Egypt in a wide range of ways. Often worn as an amulet it was also said to improve vision, both physically and psychically and to be useful in the treatment of diseases of the eye. Ground to a powder it was used as a pigment in paint and as a vivid green eye makeup.

In Italy, during the Middle Ages, malachite was believed to protect the wearer from the power of the "evil eye" and has even been attributed with the power to repel lightning strikes.

Its relative softness and beautiful coloring has made it popular for carving, and throughout history malachite has been used for ornamental objects. Malachite is a stone that will lose its luster if used frequently for healing as it absorbs negativity. It should be cleansed and recharged frequently by being placed on a cluster of clear quartz or amethyst for a few hours.

MOONSTONE

PHYSICAL HEALING: THE MOONSTONE ASSISTS THE BODY IN FINDING HORMONAL BALANCE AND IS OFTEN CONSIDERED TO BE A WOMEN'S STONE. IT IS USEFUL TO WOMEN DURING THE TIMES OF TRANSITION IN THEIR LIVES: FROM GIRL TO YOUNG WOMAN, FROM YOUNG WOMAN TO MOTHER, FROM MOTHER TO "WISE WOMAN".

EMOTIONS: MOONSTONE ENABLES BOTH MEN AND WOMEN TO RECONNECT TO THE FEMININE ASPECT OF THEIR NATURES, THUS MAKING IT EASIER FOR THEM TO ACCESS THEIR INTUITION AND NURTURING PARTS.

MENTAL/SPIRITUAL GROWTH: AN EXCELLENT MEDITATION STONE, MOONSTONE OPENS US UP TO SEE OUR PLACE IN RELATIONSHIP TO THE WORLD AROUND US. IT CAN ALSO ASSIST THE LETTING GO OF OLD OR NEGATIVE SITUATIONS OR BEHAVIOR PATTERNS TO ALLOW NEW BEHAVIOR PATTERNS OR CIRCUMSTANCES TO ESTABLISH THEMSELVES IN OUR LIVES.

CHAKRAS: BALANCES BROW CHAKRA AND OPENS CROWN CHAKRA.

ZODIAC AFFINITIES: CANCER, SCORPIO.

BIRTHSTONE: JUNE.

The finest and bluest moonstones, according to Sinhalese legend, are found washed up by the tides every "third seventh year" when the sun and moon are in their most positive aspects. Legend also has it that the luster of these stones would increase and lessen with the waxing and waning of the moon.

In India it is considered a sacred stone.

Moonstone is a form of feldspar containing potassium and sodium. It is a translucent, milky stone with a bluish sheen and is sometimes known as water opals. Fortunately, it is not only the stones found every twenty one years that are beautiful and bestowed with healing properties.

Moonstone is said to remind us of the cyclical nature of life and to reconnect us with this ebb and flow.

OBSIDIAN

PHYSICAL HEALING: TRADITIONALLY, OBSIDIAN IS BELIEVED TO BE A PROTECTOR OF THE PHYSICAL BODY AND WAS BELIEVED TO BE ABLE TO NEUTRALIZE SNAKE VENOM AND REMOVE OTHER TOXINS FROM THE BODY.

EMOTIONS: SAID TO REFLECT NEGATIVITY, OBSIDIAN ALSO KEEPS OUR EMOTIONAL STATE GROUNDED AND STABLE, ALLOWING US TO "REGAIN OUR FEET" AFTER UNUSUALLY STRESSFUL EVENTS.

MENTAL/SPIRITUAL GROWTH: OBSIDIAN IS OFTEN USED FOR CRYSTAL GAZING WITH EITHER POLISHED BALLS OR OBSIDIAN "MIRRORS" BEING USED. AS A HEALING STONE IT IS CONSIDERED BY MOST A POWERFUL STONE TO BE USED WITH RESPECT AND RESERVE. IT CAN PROVIDE POTENT INSIGHTS BUT MAY BRING THESE TO OUR CONSCIOUS MIND IN A VERY DIRECT, UNSUBTLE WAY WHICH MAY BE OVERWHELMING. OBSIDIAN'S GLASSY SURFACE IS SAID TO REFLECT BACK TO US OUR FAULTS AND SHORTCOMINGS.

CHAKRAS: BALANCES BASE CHAKRA.

ZODIAC AFFINITIES: ARIES AND AQUARIUS.

BIRTHSTONE: SEPTEMBER.

Obsidian is formed from the lava flow of volcanic eruptions and is often described as "volcanic glass" since it is created so quickly that it does not have time to form facets. It is a fairly fragile stone and when broken can form sharp edges; this quality made it popular among ancient peoples as it made excellent spear heads, arrow heads and knives, and many ancient tools are still found today, illustrating its durability.

There is a surprising variation in color for such a dark, glassy stone. Obsidian can be found with surface sheens of blue, green, black, red, gold, and purple; it can also be found with a snowflake pattern of white on its surface indicating the presence of the mineral phenocryst during its formation.

ONYX, WHITE

PHYSICAL HEALING: ONYX IS A STRENGTHENING STONE AND TONES THE HEART AND BLOOD VESSELS IMPROVING CIRCULATION TO THE EXTREMITIES OF THE BODY. ONYX IS TRADITIONALLY SAID TO IMPROVE THE CONDITION OF THE HAIR AND NAILS AND TO DRIVE OUT FROM THE BODY ANY IMPURITIES.

EMOTIONS: ENHANCING SELF-DISCIPLINE, ONYX IS A USEFUL STONE FOR THOSE WHO FEEL THEIR LIFE IS RULED BY THEIR PASSIONS AND DESIRES. ONYX ALSO INSTILLS A POSITIVE OUTLOOK, ASSISTS IN LIFTING MILD DEPRESSION AND IN COMBATING STRESS.

MENTAL/SPIRITUAL GROWTH: ONYX IS A CRYSTAL OF CONCENTRATION AND OF INSPIRATION MAKING IT A PERFECT STONE FOR MEDITATION AND FOR GAINING PERSONAL INSIGHTS. OFTEN USED IN ROSARY BEADS, IT IS ALSO CONSIDERED TO BE A STONE OF DEVOTION.

CHAKRAS: BALANCES CROWN CHAKRA.

ZODIAC AFFINITIES: LEO.

Greek legend tells the story of how white onyx came to form as a stone. Cupid, using the sharp edge of his arrowhead, cut the fingernails of Venus as she lay sleeping. These divine clippings fell into the river Indus; sinking to the bottom of the river, they transformed into white onyx.

During the Middle Ages, onyx of all colors was thought to bring misfortune to its owner and could only safely be worn if accompanied by a piece of sard (carnelian). Traditionally the stone was said to bring on disturbing dreams, although it was believed to cure epilepsy.

Onyx is a form of chalcedony. It is not only found as a white stone, but also occurs as a black stone as well as in layered combinations of black, white, red and golden brown.

ROSE QUARTZ

PHYSICAL HEALING: LINKED TO THE HEART CHAKRA ON AN ENERGY LEVEL, ROSE QUARTZ IS ALSO USEFUL IN HEALING THE PHYSICAL HEART — ITS WARM, COMFORTING COLOR EASES HEART PAIN AND LOWERS HIGH BLOOD PRESSURE. THE GENTLE INFLUENCE OF ROSE QUARTZ ALSO MAKES IT AN IDEAL CRYSTAL FOR CHILDREN AND ADOLESCENTS TO USE, BOOSTING THEIR SELF-ESTEEM AND THEIR ABILITY TO EXPRESS THEIR NEEDS.

EMOTIONS: ROSE QUARTZ IS BENEFICIAL WHEREVER THERE HAS BEEN LOSS OR TRAUMA OF ANY KIND. A COMFORTING STONE, IT CAN FACILITATE THE EXPRESSION OF ANGER IN A SAFE WAY AND SOFTEN THE PAIN OF GRIEVING. ROSE QUARTZ ENCOURAGES US TO BE LESS DEMANDING OF OURSELVES.

MENTAL/SPIRITUAL GROWTH: ROSE QUARTZ IMBUES US WITH A SENSE OF LOVE AND COMPASSION FOR OTHERS, GIVING US A GREATER UNDERSTANDING OF THE DIFFICULTIES THEY MAY BE EXPERIENCING. IT ENCOURAGES FORGIVENESS AND HELPS US DEVELOP TRUST AND ACCEPTANCE.

CHAKRAS: OPENS AND BALANCES THE HEART CHAKRA.

ZODIAC AFFINITIES: LIBRA, VIRGO AND TAURUS.

A Gift for Love

Rose quartz is a powerful expression of love. It may be given to people born under any sign of the zodiac, and will have a powerful effect on whoever receives it. A particularly good gift for children, encouraging a nurturing and compassionate spirit.

Rose quartz is clear quartz crystal that has formed in the presence of either magnesium or titanium. The color varies from the vaguest suggestion of pink to a rose pink that is translucent rather than clear. Rose quartz is most commonly found as masses or as chunks cut from a vein of rose quartz, some of which can be enormous in size. It is also available as tumbled stones, cut and polished into pyramids and spheres. More rarely, rose quartz is found in clusters or as single terminated stones; these are, however, significantly more expensive than the masses, as are examples of rutilated rose quartz.

When cleansing rose quartz, it should be noted that it will lose its color if exposed to the sun for long periods of time. For this reason, cleansing with water or in a moon bath is preferable.

Rose quartz has always been linked with the heart and with love. Its influence is not confined, however, to romantic love, but to unconditional love, love of self, and spiritual love. It increases the ability to receive love from another and opens the heart chakra to allow love to be more easily expressed outwardly.

Rose quartz is said to awaken the eye and the soul to beauty It also awakens the conscious mind to old emotional traumas, allowing them to be acknowledged and healed. If the need for greater love or emotional healing is felt, it is recommended that a piece of rose quartz be worn as pendant over the heart. In this way, its influence is constantly present.

In healing, clear quartz will magnify the power of the rose quartz, so the two can be used together.

SELENITE

PHYSICAL HEALING: SELENITE HAS A HIGH CALCIUM CONTENT AND ITS INFLUENCE ASSISTS BONE TO HEAL AND STRENGTHEN. THIS INFLUENCE ALSO WORKS ON A CELLULAR LEVEL TO ENCOURAGE CELL GENERATION AND TO IMPROVE THE QUALITY OF CELLS. SELENITE, SECURED IN A POUCH AND WORN AROUND THE NECK, WAS ONCE USED TO ENSURE MOTHERS A PLENTIFUL SUPPLY OF BREAST MILK.

EMOTIONS: SELENITE CALMS THE EMOTIONS AND CAN HELP BALANCE THOSE WHO SWING BETWEEN THE EXTREMES OF THE EMOTIONS. SELENITE ENCOURAGES US TO FOCUS ON THE POSITIVE RATHER THAN THE NEGATIVE; IT EASES EMOTIONAL PAIN, DISPELLING FEARS AND UNFOUNDED ANXIETIES.

MENTAL/SPIRITUAL GROWTH: SAID TO PROVIDE ACCESS TO IMAGES AND THOUGHTS FROM FUTURE AND PAST LIVES DURING MEDITATIONS, SELENITE ENABLES US TO EXPAND OUR MENTAL ABILITIES AND PROVIDES MENTAL CLARITY.

CHAKRAS: STIMULATES THE CROWN CHAKRA.

ZODIAC AFFINITIES: TAURUS.

Under the influence of Selene, goddess of the full moon, selenite is a crystallized form of gypsum. One variety of selenite is known as the "desert rose" because the crystals form in a cluster that looks remarkably like a flower. There are many other shapes into which selenite develops, such as blades that intersect at right angles, tree shapes, clusters, and balls of crescent-shaped crystal formations. Selenite can also be found in a range of colors including clear translucent white, opaque snowy white, pink, and a crystal the color of desert sand. Selenite is a very soft stone and needs to be handled with care.

SMOKY QUARTZ

PHYSICAL HEALING: THE VIBRATION OF SMOKY QUARTZ ASSISTS THE BODY'S DIGESTIVE SYSTEM BY IMPROVING THE ABSORPTION OF VITAL NUTRIENTS AND HELPING THE BODY ELIMINATE WASTES EFFICIENTLY. SMOKY QUARTZ IS ALSO SAID TO INCREASE FERTILITY AND BALANCE OUR SEXUAL ENERGY.

EMOTIONS: THIS CRYSTAL IS A GROUNDING STONE AND IS USEFUL IN CALMING ANXIETIES AND HYPERACTIVITY. USED SPARINGLY IT CAN HELP LIFT BAD MOODS AND MILD DEPRESSIONS BY DISPELLING NEGATIVE THOUGHTS.

MENTAL/SPIRITUAL GROWTH: SMOKY QUARTZ EXPOSES THE INCONSISTENCIES BETWEEN OUR BELIEFS AND OUR ACTIONS AND AFFORDS THE OPPORTUNITY FOR CONSCIOUS CHANGE. IT CAN ALSO ELICIT OUR DEEPER COURAGE TO TRY AGAIN WHEN OUR EFFORTS AT CHANGE HAVE FAILED.

CHAKRAS: BALANCES THE BASE AND SOLAR PLEXUS CHAKRAS.

ZODIAC AFFINITIES: CAPRICORN AND SAGITTARIUS.

Smoky quartz occurs when clear quartz crystal has formed in the presence of iron or titanium. Its color can range from being just a hint of golden smokiness to a rich bronze-black. The lightest of the smoky quartz is sometimes called smoky topaz or cairngorm, and the darkest, a very black crystal, is called morion and was traditionally a stone of mourning. Rutile inclusions (see Clear Quartz) are sometimes present and these are said to increase the healing qualities of the crystal. Considered a stone of good fortune, smoky quartz was often given to soldiers going in to battle to protect them and was also carried by people in ordinary life as a talisman. If choosing for healing work, a natural stone is preferable over the smoky quartz which is artificially produced by irradiating clear quartz. These "created" stones have a tendency to be blackened in places and to have lost their translucent quality.

TIGER'S EYE

PHYSICAL HEALING: THIS CRYSTAL BALANCES THE ENERGY OF THE PHYSICAL BODY, AND CAN BE USEFUL WHEN THE BODY IS TRYING TO RID ITSELF OF TOXINS. TRADITIONALLY IT HAS ALSO BEEN USED TO IMPROVE VISION, BOTH PHYSICALLY AND PSYCHICALLY.

EMOTIONS: TIGER'S EYE INDUCES US TO MAINTAIN A POSITIVE OUTLOOK, PROVIDING OPTIMISM AND SELF-ASSURANCE. IT BALANCES THE EMOTIONS AND LESSENS MOOD SWINGS.

MENTAL/SPIRITUAL GROWTH: RECOMMENDED AS A STONE FOR THOSE WHO ARE JUST BEGINNING TO BE INTERESTED IN SPIRITUAL GROWTH, THIS EARTHY STONE GENTLY AWAKENS THE INTUITION AND OPENS THE WAY TO INNER KNOWLEDGE.

CHAKRAS: BALANCES THE BASE AND SOLAR PLEXUS CHAKRAS.

ZODIAC AFFINITIES: CAPRICORN.

Tiger's eye is formed when quartz crystal replaces some of the fibers in asbestos (either blue or gold), these many "fibers" reflect the light and create an effect similar to that produced by a cat's eye. The most common tiger's eye is an iridescent combination of rich browns, creams and golds, but it can also be found in blue-gold combinations and is sometimes heat treated to produce green and red varieties. This crystal symbolizes the union of the earth (brown) with the sun (gold) and is a stone that will lift our spirits while at the same time keeping us grounded.

The crystal's resemblance to an eye prompted their use in the Middle Ages as protection from the evil eye and other external forces of evil. It is usually available polished and can be found in a variety of shapes including irregular tumbled stones, beads, spheres, egg shapes, pyramids and obelisks.

TURQUOISE

PHYSICAL HEALING: THE COOLING BLUE OF TURQUOISE WILL EASE TIRED OR INFLAMED EYES AND FEVERS. IT HELPS THE BODY RECOVER FROM ILLNESS OR DISEASE, PARTICULARLY WHERE NEW TISSUE IS BEING REGENERATED. TURQUOISE IS ALSO A PURIFYING STONE AND IS SAID TO PROTECT THE BODY FROM THE EFFECTS OF POLLUTION.

EMOTIONS: TURQUOISE IS A STONE THAT ASSISTS EXPRESSION IN ALL ITS FORMS: VERBAL EXPRESSION OF FEELINGS AND EMOTIONS, CREATIVE EXPRESSION, AND THE PHYSICAL EXPRESSION OF HOPES AND DREAMS. IT SOFTENS THE IMPACT OF TRAUMATIC EVENTS AND HELPS US STAY BALANCED AND CALM.

MENTAL/SPIRITUAL GROWTH: STRONGLY CONNECTED TO BOTH THE EARTH AND THE SKY, TURQUOISE GENERATES MENTAL CLARITY AND EXPANSION WHILE MAINTAINING THE CONNECTION WITH THE PHYSICAL. IT CONNECTS THE MENTAL AND THE SPIRITUAL ENABLING US TO UTILIZE OUR INNER KNOWLEDGE AND WISDOM IN PRACTICAL WAYS.

CHAKRAS: STIMULATES AND BALANCES HEART, THROAT AND BROW CHAKRAS.

ZODIAC AFFINITIES: SCORPIO, PISCES, CAPRICORN.

BIRTHSTONE: DECEMBER.

Traditionally, turquoise was a stone always received as a gift and never purchased; it was often a gift between lovers or to a loved one about to embark on a journey.

The ancients described turquoise as being "the blue of the desert sky" and was considered by many cultures to be a powerful stone. The ancient Egyptians believed that it would avert the evil eye, and in Tibet turquoise was considered a lucky stone, keeping its owner safe and attracting good fortune.

Some Native American tribes used turquoise to initiate rain and shamans always carried a piece of turquoise. Hindu mythology states that if you look at a piece of turquoise immediately after you have first looked at the new moon, you will become wealthy beyond measure. In Europe and in Asia it was believed to protect riders as it prevented horses and camels from stumbling — even today in the Middle East a turquoise bead is often sewn onto the trapping of a camel or the bridle of a horse. The stone was also believed to absorb the impact of a fall, thereby saving the wearer. Often the turquoise was said to split or crack as a result of this pressure. The Pueblo tribes of North America always placed a piece of turquoise under the floor whenever a house was built to ensure the well-being of those who lived within.

The color of turquoise can range from brilliant aqua blues to pale blues and greens; the veins running through turquoise might be black, brown or gold depending on the mineral present. Heat and moisture affect the color of turquoise as will any chemical with which it comes in contact. It was once believed that the color reflected the health and safety of the wearer; if the turquoise paled, there was danger or illness ahead.

THE SIGNIFICANCE OF
COLOR IN CRYSTALS

RED AND ORANGE Red and orange stones are warming and stimulating. The color of fire, they may be used wherever a body system is sluggish or the need for warmth is felt. Red stones can boost our circulation and stimulate our digestive system.
They are said to encourage fertility and connect us with our sexual energy. They can also inflame our emotions, and if anger or fear is present, they should be balanced with a soothing green stone. Red and orange stones are often used to awaken a depleted base chakra.
Red and orange crystals include: ruby, garnet, carnelian, citrine, orange calcite, red jasper.

YELLOW Yellow stones reflect the energy of the sun and can lift anxieties and mild depression in the same way a sunny day can. They are warming and stimulating, but not as "hot" as red crystals. Yellow crystals can be used to balance the solar plexus chakra; they can inspire us out of bouts of inactivity and boredom and fill us with purposeful energy. Yellow stones should be balanced with violet or deep blue stones if you are suffering from nervous exhaustion or vague anxieties. Yellow stones include: tiger's eye, citrine, calcite, yellow jade, topaz.

PINK Pink is the color of love in all its forms. It is nurturing and comforting, restful and calming. Pink inspires creativity and self-acceptance; it encourages self-esteem and softens the grieving process. Pink stones can be balanced with those of a pale green color. Pink crystals include: rose quartz, pink calcite, kunzite, pink selenite, watermelon tourmaline, rose jade, rhodochrosite.

VIOLET Violet is the color of spirituality and awareness; it is at once both energizing and calming. Violet stones are useful to those who suffer from anxiety, nervous exhaustion and the effects of stress. The brow chakra relates to these regal stones and the color is said to awaken the third eye, providing us with psychic "sight". The intensity of violet stones can be softened by yellow stones. Violet crystals include: amethyst, purple fluorite, lavender jade.

BLACK Black crystals powerfully connect us with the earth. They steady us and help us maintain our center, stabilizing our emotions. Black stones are often used at the base chakra and primarily for the physical body, but they can also stimulate an awakening of the subconscious mind. Deflecting negativity and dispelling fear and confusion, black crystals are considered to be stones of protection. Black crystals include: obsidian, black onyx, smoky quartz, hematite.

WHITE White is the color of spiritual strength, of purity and inspiration. It is the color of inner peace and of the connection we have to the universe. White stones relate to the crown chakra and are generally used for the intellect and the spirit. White stones include: moonstone, white onyx, white howlite, white jade, selenite.

GREEN AND BLUE Green is the color of new life, regeneration and healing. It is a cool, soothing color that works towards harmony. It can relieve nervous tension and assist wherever physical healing of tissue is needed.

Blue is the color of the heavens, it too is cooling and can help reduce high temperatures and draw the heat from burns and infections. It can have a calming and balancing effect on the mind and emotions. Many stones contain both blue and green and their properties are a blending of the two colors. Green stones can be balanced with red crystals and blue with orange crystals.

Green and blue stones include: aquamarine, aventurine, turquoise, chrysoprase, peridot, lapis lazuli, bloodstone, green jasper, jade.

CRYSTALS IN THE
HOME AND OFFICE

Crystals can be used in a wide variety of ways and are not restricted to healing sessions or just being an object of beauty. As you use crystals more often you will develop a greater understanding of their subtle influences so will discover even more uses for them. Here are just a few ways crystals can be applied.

IN A CHILD'S ROOM

Hang clear quartz crystal prisms in a sunny window and the room will be filled with rainbows. A light breeze can have the rainbows dancing around the room. Children love these treasures in their own spaces, but make sure the crystals are firmly secured and are out of reach of small children.

PROTECTION FROM ELECTROMAGNETIC RADIATION

Smoky quartz and amethyst are said to protect people from some of the electromagnetic radiation from computers and computer monitors and from television screens. Place a large piece of clear quartz, smoky quartz or an amethyst cluster between you and the monitor of your computer. Both amethyst and smoky quartz will stimulate your imagination, so they are a good choice if you are using your computer for creative work. Malachite has also traditionally been considered a stone that absorbs radiation. Generally, the larger the crystal, the more electromagnetic radiation it is able to absorb or repel, so don't expect too much from a tiny piece of crystal on top of a television set. It is also wise to swap the crystals around and cleanse them after they've been used for this purpose (see CARING FOR YOUR CRYSTALS, pages 12–14).

ENHANCE DRINKING WATER

Drinking water can be enhanced by charging it with a clear quartz crystal. Choose a reasonably small crystal (a large one is likely to break the jug or water container when you pour) and wash the crystal to ensure it is clean and free of dirt particles. Place it in direct sunlight for three to four hours, then rinse under running water. The crystal should now be placed in the jug of drinking water. Leave overnight and the crystal-charged water is ready to enjoy. The crystal can be left in the bottom of the container and rinsed under running water each time you refill the container. Every few weeks you may like to repeat the initial process to recharge the quartz.

RELIEVE A STRESSFUL ENVIRONMENT

If your workplace is a stressful environment with several conflicting personalities, try placing a large piece of rose quartz with a clear quartz cluster in a strategic position. The rose quartz assists the environment by allowing

everyone to consider the feelings of others and the clear
quartz amplifies the effect of the rose quartz and also
helps balance the energy in the room. Fluorite is a valuable
crystal to keep on your desk as it fosters the ability to think
in a structured, focused and logical way. Azurite enhances
mental clarity and assists in decision making.

CRYSTAL MASSAGE

To make a crystal-enhanced massage oil, find a thick-walled glass bottle with a
mouth wide enough to take your crystals. The crystals you use should be
tumbled stones as these are the least likely to chip or leave fragments in the oil.
Choose crystals that have appropriate characteristics for your purpose, for
example, amethyst makes a relaxing massage oil, whereas carnelian will make
a warming and stimulating oil. Half fill the bottle with a high quality massage
oil such as cold pressed apricot or sweet almond oil. Tilt the bottle and gently
slide two or three crystals into the oil. Fill the bottle to the top and place in
direct sunshine for a few hours. Leave for two to three days and the oil will be
ready for massage.

FOR A CREATIVE ENVIRONMENT

If your work requires you to be creative and mentally alert, an amethyst geode
or cluster will ensure your working environment provides
you with stimulation. Aquamarine and turquoise are
crystals that facilitate expression and can be useful to those
who have creative ideas but find it difficult
to express them.

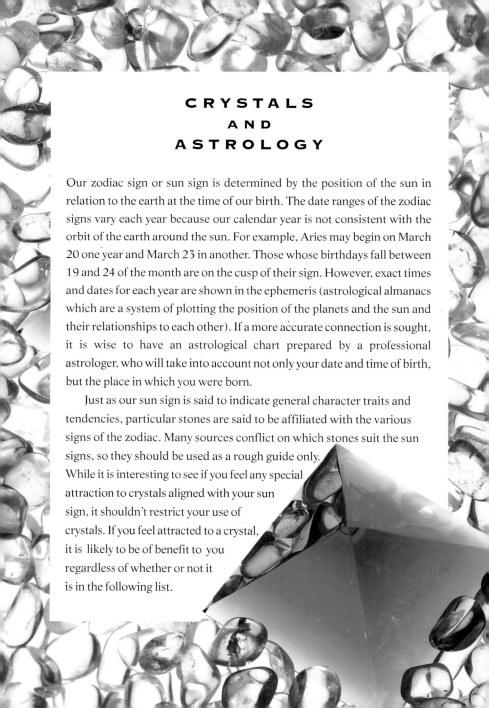

CRYSTALS
AND
ASTROLOGY

Our zodiac sign or sun sign is determined by the position of the sun in relation to the earth at the time of our birth. The date ranges of the zodiac signs vary each year because our calendar year is not consistent with the orbit of the earth around the sun. For example, Aries may begin on March 20 one year and March 23 in another. Those whose birthdays fall between 19 and 24 of the month are on the cusp of their sign. However, exact times and dates for each year are shown in the ephemeris (astrological almanacs which are a system of plotting the position of the planets and the sun and their relationships to each other). If a more accurate connection is sought, it is wise to have an astrological chart prepared by a professional astrologer, who will take into account not only your date and time of birth, but the place in which you were born.

Just as our sun sign is said to indicate general character traits and tendencies, particular stones are said to be affiliated with the various signs of the zodiac. Many sources conflict on which stones suit the sun signs, so they should be used as a rough guide only. While it is interesting to see if you feel any special attraction to crystals aligned with your sun sign, it shouldn't restrict your use of crystals. If you feel attracted to a crystal, it is likely to be of benefit to you regardless of whether or not it is in the following list.

ARIES
🐏 The Ram — March 20 to April 20
Aquamarine, aventurine, clear quartz,
hematite, lapis lazuli, malachite, obsidian

TAURUS
🐂 The Bull — April 21 to May 19
Carnelian, clear quartz, jade,
rose quartz, selenite

GEMINI
👯 The Twins — May 20 to June 20
Blue lace agate, aquamarine,
clear quartz, jade

CANCER
🦀 The Crab — June 21 to July 21
Aventurine, carnelian,
clear quartz, moonstone

LEO
🦁 The Lion — July 22 to August 21
Carnelian, citrine, clear quartz,
jasper, white onyx

VIRGO
👩 The Virgin — August 22 to September 21
Clear quartz,
carnelian, agate

LIBRA
The Scales — September 22 to Scorpio 22
Aventurine, chrysoprase, citrine, clear quartz,
jade, moonstone, rose quartz

SCORPIO
The Scorpion — October 23 to November 21
Clear quartz, labradorite,
moonstone, turquoise

SAGITTARIUS
The Archer — November 22 to December 20
Amethyst, azurite, clear quartz, labradorite,
obsidian, smoky quartz, turquoise

CAPRICORN
The Goat — December 21 to January 19
Amethyst, clear quartz, fluorite,
smoky quartz, tiger's eye

AQUARIUS
The Water-bearer — January 20 to February 17
Azurite, clear quartz,
hematite, lapis lazuli

PISCES
Fishes — February 18 to March 19
Amethyst, blue lace agate, chrysoprase,
clear quartz, fluorite, turquoise

BIRTHSTONES

Although the concept of birthstones has been in use since biblical times, it was only during the eighteenth century that the practice of wearing birthstones became popular. The allocation of a stone to each month of the year rose from the influences of astrology, the zodiac in particular, and also to gems representing the twelve apostles. It is also believed that originally the stone would be worn during its month and then replaced by the next month's stone, rather than the birth month stone being worn all year.

JANUARY ~ garnet

FEBRUARY ~ amethyst

MARCH ~ aquamarine, bloodstone

APRIL ~ diamond, zircon

MAY ~ emerald, tourmaline, chrysoprase

JUNE ~ pearl, moonstone

JULY ~ ruby, carnelian

AUGUST ~ peridot, sardonyx

SEPTEMBER ~ sapphire, lapis lazuli

OCTOBER ~ opal

NOVEMBER ~ topaz

DECEMBER ~ turquoise

CRYSTALS
AND THE
CHAKRAS

THE CHAKRA SYSTEM

The chakras represent energy centers and give us a system through which we can understand the constant flow of energy through and around our bodies. The word chakra comes from the Sanskrit for "wheel" and chakras have been studied and written about for centuries in the East, and more recently in the Western world. As often occurs with knowledge that is very old and drawn from many sources, there is much conflicting information on chakras. Most systems, however, recognize that there are many chakras. The seven discussed below are considered the main chakras.

BASE CHAKRA

This first chakra may also be called the root chakra or the sexual chakra and is located at the base of the spine. It is represented in ancient Hindu texts as a lotus with four petals. The corresponding color for this chakra is red.

This energy center is linked with our instinct to survive; it relates to the physical rather than the emotional. It is the source of courage to stand and fight or the stamina and energy to take flight when our survival is threatened. From the base chakra comes the sexual energy to reproduce and ensure the survival of our species. If our concerns in life center around where our next meal is coming from or how we are going to pay the rent, our base chakra will dominate. This chakra also represents our connection with the earth.

Crystals for the base chakra include: obsidian, smoky quartz, hematite, carnelian, red jasper, garnet, clear quartz.

BELLY CHAKRA

This second chakra is also known as the sacral plexus and is located approximately midway between the base of the spine and the navel. It is represented in ancient Hindu texts as a lotus with six petals. The corresponding color for this chakra is orange.

This chakra is the source of our creative energy and is associated with our emotions, our intuition and our sexuality. It is the source of our desires and passions and our connection with the element of water.

Crystals for the belly chakra include: carnelian, citrine, tiger's eye, clear quartz.

SOLAR PLEXUS CHAKRA

The third chakra is located just above the navel and is the chakra that relates to how we interact with the world around us. It is represented in ancient Hindu texts as a lotus with ten petals. The corresponding color for this chakra is yellow. The solar plexus chakra is the source of our energy to act, it is the source of our personal power. Through the solar plexus we are able transform our desires and emotions into action. The solar plexus is the point of intersection between the physical and the mental. Crystals for the solar plexus chakra include: tiger's eye, malachite, hematite, jasper, citrine, clear quartz.

HEART CHAKRA

The fourth chakra is located in the center of the body at the level of the heart. It is represented in ancient Hindu texts as a lotus with twelve petals. The corresponding color for this chakra is green.

As its name implies, this chakra is the source of our love, not just romantic or sexual love, but unconditional love of those around us along with a sense of

community beyond our own needs. It is the source of our compassion and understanding. The heart chakra is involved with our sense of relationship, how we relate to others, our place in the world and how all other things relate to each other and to ourselves.

Crystals for the heart chakra include: rose quartz, aventurine, jade, chrysoprase, watermelon tourmaline, rhodochrosite, clear quartz.

THROAT CHAKRA

The fifth chakra is located at the throat. It is represented in ancient Hindu texts as a lotus with sixteen petals. The corresponding color for this chakra is pale blue. This is the chakra of communication. It is involved with how we express ourselves in the world, both verbally and non-verbally and how we receive information from the world. The throat chakra is involved with the silent communications that happen within our body, the nervous system and the endocrine system.

Crystals for the throat chakra include: turquoise, aquamarine, lapis lazuli, azurite, jasper, clear quartz.

BROW CHAKRA

The sixth chakra is located at the center of the forehead. This chakra is also known as the third eye chakra. It is represented in ancient Hindu texts as a lotus with two petals. The corresponding color for this chakra is indigo.

Through our third eye we gain insight and a deeper level of understanding. The information received is not received visually, it is perceived. Developing the energy at this chakra involves an increased level of awareness thereby enabling us to access our inner wisdom.

Crystals for the brow chakra include: lapis lazuli, moonstone, fluorite, clear quartz.

CROWN CHAKRA

The seventh chakra is located at the top of the head. It is represented in ancient Hindu texts as a lotus with a thousand petals. The corresponding color for this chakra is purple.

The crown chakra is the source of our thoughts, our conscious and unconscious minds, our beliefs and dreams. It connects to our inner sense of "knowing" and is the intersecting point between our mind and our body.

Crystals for the crown chakra include: amethyst, moonstone, fluorite, clear quartz.

HEALING with CRYSTALS

It is widely accepted that all living things are surrounded by electro-magnetic energy and that the particles making up these life forms constantly vibrate. Crystals also vibrate and Kirlian photography has demonstrated that all crystals have an individual "signature" electro-magnetic field.

Kirlian photography has also been able to capture the increased energy emitted from the body when someone is holding a piece of quartz crystal. It appears that when a crystal is held, it begins to resonate with our individual frequency, thus increasing the energy in our bodies.

Research into how crystals work therapeutically is being carried out in many places throughout the world. There is some evidence to suggest that crystals resonate with the frequency of healthy cells, drawing unhealthy cells that may be vibrating at a lower or higher frequency back into the normal range by a process called "entrainment".

Since every cell in our body has its own frequency, this may explain why some crystals will work most effectively on a particular part of the body and why not every crystal will be beneficial to any one person.

When deciding which stones to use for healing and where they should be placed on the body, the chapters A–Z of Crystals and Crystals and the Chakras will provide some guidance, but also trust your intuition If you instinctively feel you would like to use a particular stone or feel drawn to it when thinking about a particular part of the body, use the crystal and judge the results for yourself. If you don't have a piece of a crystal specified in the chakra layout below, look to crystals of a similar color. While it is easier to use the following crystal layouts on another person, it is also possible to use them on yourself.

To balance the chakras

Before you begin a crystal healing session make sure all the crystals you are about to use have been cleansed (see CARING FOR YOUR CRYSTALS, pages 12–14) and are all at hand. If any haven't been cleansed, use a simple, short meditation to imagine any negativity falling away from the crystal, leaving it clear, clean and vibrant. Take a few moments to center yourself and bring your focus to the layout.

Lie on your back (or have the person you are working with lie on their back) and slowly put the crystals into position as described below. Stay in this position while you breathe deeply and slowly for about 15 minutes.

Slowly remove the crystals, starting at the crown and working downwards. Take your time getting up and have a drink of cool, but not iced, water.

Crown chakra

Place a single terminated clear quartz crystal or a tumbled quartz crystal a short distance away from the top of the head. If using a terminated crystal, angle the point towards the head — this directs energy into the crown chakra.

Brow chakra

Place a single point of amethyst, a piece of tumbled amethyst or purple fluorite over the brow chakra.

THROAT CHAKRA

For the throat chakra use a piece of aquamarine or jade on
the throat, over the voice box.

HEART CHAKRA

Place a small piece of uncut or tumbled rose quartz crystal
over the heart chakra.

SOLAR PLEXUS

Place a single point, a small cluster or a tumbled piece of
citrine over the solar plexus. If using a terminated crystal,
position so the point of the stone is facing toward the head
or facing upwards, away from the body.

BELLY CHAKRA

Place a piece of carnelian or red jasper halfway between the
solar plexus and the base of the spine.

BASE CHAKRA

Place a single point or tumbled stone of smoky quartz over
the base of the spine. If using a terminated crystal, position
so the point of the stone is facing towards to the head.

CRYSTAL
MEDITATION

The qualities of crystals can intensify a meditation, enhancing the connection we make to the place within ourselves that is calm and peaceful. If you are only just beginning to meditate, it may be useful to select a stone that encourages a tranquil mind, such as amethyst, azurite or purple fluorite. If you are meditating regularly, be aware of the purpose of your meditation and choose a crystal with qualities that will support that purpose. For example, if you are seeking to become more trusting of your intuition, chrysoprase would be a good choice, whereas if you are meditating to find clarity of mind, carnelian would be more appropriate.

Find a space to meditate in which you will be comfortable and undisturbed; this may be inside or outdoors. Ensure the clothing you are wearing is loose and warm enough to prevent you feeling cold when sitting still for a length of time.

Imagine a square around you. At each corner of the square, place a single terminating quartz crystal with the terminated end pointing toward you. Then take the crystal you have especially chosen, and cradle it in your open hands. The four quartz crystals will focus energy toward you and will increase the properties of the crystal you are holding. This crystal meditation can be used to determine how a crystal will be beneficial to you.

Sit or lie in a comfortable position, slowly bring your focus to your breath. As you breathe in, imagine your body filling with clear, clean air and as you breathe out imagine all tension, stress and negativity leaving your body. As you begin to feel more relaxed and your body feels heavy, turn your attention to the crystal.

Become aware of how it feels in your hands, whether it feels cool or warm, heavy or light, vibrant or dull. Does the crystal feel energizing or sedating? As you are doing this, imagine the color of the crystal slowly rising in a mist from the crystal and surrounding you.

Take notice of how this feels. Do you feel comfortable or stressed, safe or anxious, stimulated or depleted? If you know the chakra to which the crystal relates (see CRYSTALS AND THE CHAKRAS, pages 64–67), you may like to hold the crystal for a time in front of this chakra and be conscious of any sensations.

Allow any images that come up to gradually develop in your mind's eye. This may not happen the first time you meditate with your crystal, and take into account that everyone receives information in their own unique way. Some people will see images as if on film, others may hear an inner voice while others may gain insight by grasping abstract concepts.

Ask any questions that come to mind and be open to an answer appearing in some way. No information you gain from the crystal in this way is "right" or "wrong" and different people will interact with the same crystal in different ways.

Once you feel the time is right, gently place the crystal on the ground in front of you. Bring your focus back to your breath and slowly bring your attention to the outside world, taking all the time you feel you need. You may like to record your experience by speaking into a tape or by starting a crystal journal.

USING CRYSTALS FOR PREDICTION

CRYSTAL GAZING

Crystal gazing or scrying as a means of divination is an ancient tradition. Crystal balls have long been associated with fortune telling and although the crystals portrayed in pictures of the stereotypical gypsy are of clear quartz crystal, traditionally the most commonly used crystal for scrying was beryl. Of the beryls, aquamarine with its pale, watery blue-green coloring was favored. Astrologically, this stone was believed to be strongly influenced by the moon, and scryers would only attempt divination when the moon was on the increase.

Crystal balls are now made from a wide range of crystals. Though expensive, modern cutting and polishing techniques and an increase in mining have reduced the monetary value of these crystals significantly.

If you would like to try crystal gazing for yourself, choose a crystal ball large enough to fit comfortably in your cupped hand. Find a quiet space in a dimly lit room, drape a piece of dark cloth over your hand and place the crystal on top. Take a few minutes to relax and breathe deeply. Slowly bring your focus to the crystal ball and look into its depths. Relax your eyes and be aware of when you begin the attempt to "see", then relax again. During this time maintain your mental focus on a subject you would like clarified. At first, try crystal gazing for short periods of time only, to avoid eye strain. Gradually increase the time you spend gazing, always staying within a time comfortable for your eyes. Crystal gazers speak of a "clouding" that occurs just before images appear, so if this occurs, you are almost there!

USING A PENDULUM

Using a pendulum is perhaps the easiest way to use crystals for prediction. Many New Age stores sell crystal pendulums already made, but it's not a difficult task to make your own.

Choosing a crystal is the most important part. Ideally, you should choose a crystal you feel a connection with, but keep in mind that it also needs to move evenly, so a crystal with a balanced point will make the most effective pendulum. It should also be relatively small, enabling easy movement.

Once you've chosen your crystal, a string, chain or leather thong needs to be attached to its base. This can be done by gluing a metal cap onto it and attaching the string to this, or by binding the base tightly with leather or string and connecting two strands to the binding. The two strands are then joined with a knot close to the base of the crystal and at the ends. When completed, the pendulum should point straight downwards.

A pendulum will swing with three different movements: anti-clockwise, clockwise and side to side. The first step in using your pendulum is to establish which movement means "yes", which means "no" and which means "don't know". Hold the pendulum and wait until all movement has stopped. Ask a question whose answer you know, without doubt, is "yes".

The pendulum should begin to slowly move and after a few moments, a clear pattern of movement should be established. This is your movement for "yes". Repeat the process to discover the movement for "no". The remaining option will indicate "don't know". If you receive this answer it may mean there are many possible answers or you need to rephrase the question. To use a pendulum effectively it is necessary always to phrase your question so it can be answered by "yes" or "no".

CASTING THE STONES

Casting stones is another method that can be used for prediction and involves taking a handful of different types of crystals and stones, and scattering them on the ground or on a table in front of you. The position of the stones and their position in relation to the others are then interpreted to foretell future events. There are many different systems and a variety of methods for reading the stones once they have been cast. Some systems work within a circle and some work on any flat surface; some systems will give the caster a choice of crystals and those that are rejected are equal in significance to those that are cast. Other systems may look for a picture formed by the stones, while some may see the stones as a symbol for something else and predict according to the stories behind these.

While many of these systems take a great deal of practice and dedication to interpret the stones with any accuracy, there is a simple form of casting that can be used to find answers to "yes" or "no" questions.

To use this method choose three tumble polished crystals of different colors — unpolished stones are likely to be damaged. Choose one to be the key stone. Hold the stones loosely in your hand, shake them lightly and hold the word "yes" in your mind. Gently cast them onto the ground or onto a table.

Look at the position in which the stones have fallen. The stone nearest the key stone is your "yes/true" stone and the stone farthest from the key stone is the "no/false" stone.

You can now ask any question that can be answered with "yes", "no", "true" or "false", cast the stones and interpret the answer. If your "yes/true" stone is further away from the key stone than the "no/false" stone then the answer is "no" and vice versa. If the "yes/true" and "no/false" stones are equal distances from the key stone, the answer can be interpreted as "I don't know".

CONCLUSION

If you use the power of crystals as outlined in this book, you will be able to access their power to alter your moods and develop your spiritual and psychic selves. They will give you the energy and courage for difficult undertakings or help you mend a broken heart. Their influence can also help your body recover from illness and assist in focusing your energy toward the healing of others.

When you visit a crystal shop try to do so when time is not a priority. Then you have the freedom to either choose your crystals or let them choose you. The wonders of light, color, shape and texture you encounter there will only be the beginning of a magical experience that will continue for the rest of your life.

Some terms were used in this book that might have been unfamiliar to you. Here is a short explanation of these for your quick reference:

chalcedony – a type of quartz with a very small crystalline structure. Examples include jasper, agate and tiger's eye.

geode– a piece of rock with a cavity lined with crystals.

nodule – a relatively small, rounded piece of stone in a non-crystalline form.

amulet – a charm or piece of jewelry worn specifically to protect the wearer from evil forces and physical harm.

talisman – a stone worn or carried to attract good fortune, luck, love and happiness.

smudge stick – stalks of sage (or other herbs) tied together which are lit and the smoke used to purify a space or object.

piezoelectrical field – the electrical field produced when certain types of crystals are placed under mechanical stress.

beryl– a mineral composed of beryllium aluminium silicate. Found in green, blue, pink, white and yellow.

chakra – an energy center of the body. Through the chakras the body receives and transmits the life energy.

mica – a broad term applied to a group of minerals containing hydrous silicates of aluminium or potassium. They have a lustrous, light reflecting quality.

pseudomorphus – the process of one mineral replacing and taking on the crystalline shape of another mineral.

stalagmite – a conical mass of calcium carbonate rising up from the floor of a cave.

stalagtite – a conical mass of calcium carbonate descending from the ceiling of a cave.

octahedrons – a solid with eight faces.

feldspar – a name give to rocks that contain aluminium silicates of potassium, sodium, calcium or barium. Some examples are: moonstone, labradorite and spectrolite.

pyrites – consist of disulphides of iron, copper or tin. Iron pyrite is also known as 'fools gold'.

Kirlian photography – a techique of photography developed by Semyan and Valentina Kirlian. It captures on photographic film the electrical field that radiates from organic matter.

scrying – to divine or predict events.

INDEX TO CRYSTAL HEALING

DISCLAIMER

This book is intended to give general information only and is not substitute
for professional and medical advice. The publisher, author and distributor
expressly disclaim all liability to any person arising directly or indirectly from
the use of, or for any errors or omissions in, the information in this book.
The adoption and application of the information in this book is at the reader's
discretion and is their sole responsibility.

COPYRIGHT © LANSDOWNE PUBLISHING PTY LTD

PUBLISHED BY LANSDOWNE PUBLISHING PTY LTD
SYDNEY, AUSTRALIA

CEO Steven Morris
email: steven@lansdownepublishing.com.au

FIRST PUBLISHED 1997

REPRINTED 1999, 2000, 2003, 2005
THIS EDITION 2014

EDITOR: CYNTHIA BLANCHE
DESIGNER: LIZ SEYMOUR
SET IN LIFE ON QUARKXPRESS

PRINTED IN SINGAPORE
BY TIEN WAH PRESS (PTE) LTD

NATIONAL LIBRARY OF AUSTRALIA
CATALOGUING-IN-PUBLICATION DATA

TOY, FIONA
THE BOOK OF CRYSTALS.

INCLUDES INDEX.
ISBN 1 86302 720 3.
ISBN 9781863027205.

1. CRYSTALS. 2. CRYSTALS – THERAPEUTIC USE.
3, CRYSTALS – PSYCHIC ASPECTS I. TITLE.

133.2548